EXPLOR...
OCEAN

by Gail Blasser Riley   *illustrated by* Michael Maydak

MODERN CURRICULUM PRESS
Pearson Learning Group

Have you ever walked along the seashore collecting sea shells, pieces of polished glass, or bits of driftwood? If so, you know that the ocean holds many interesting treasures. Have you ever wondered about what lives in the ocean?

More plants and animals live in the oceans than anywhere else on Earth. That is because the ocean is an ideal environment for many different plants and animals. The temperature is comfortable. And it is easy to move in water.

Let's begin our exploration near the shore—in the shallow, soft sea bed.

3

You may have difficulty seeing some of the creatures in the shallow sea bed. That's because many of them burrow their way into the sand.

If you look carefully, you might catch sight of a sea pen. The sea pen is an animal that looks like an old feather writing pen. The sea pen uses tiny buds on its "feather" to catch small creatures that float by. The buds are sharp, like burrs on land plants.

Other interesting animals of the sea bed are clams, crabs, and seahorses. You can follow the eagle ray to find them. The eagle ray finds its dinner with its snout. After eating some clams, crabs, or seahorses, the eagle ray may also dig out worms and flatfish from the sand.

Flatfish

Peacock Worm

Clam

Worm

You probably don't want to find some of the creatures that live on the shallow sea bed. Be wary of creatures like the weaver fish. It has poison that it uses to protect itself.

Most of the worms on the sea bed are not at all dangerous. One such worm is the bristle worm. (It is also called a sea mouse.) This creature is covered with bristles that are like hair. That's what led people to give it its two names. The peacock worm gets its name from the way it looks too. Its tentacles fan out so it looks like a peacock. These tentacles quickly disappear into the worm's tubes if a hungry flatfish comes by looking for a snack.

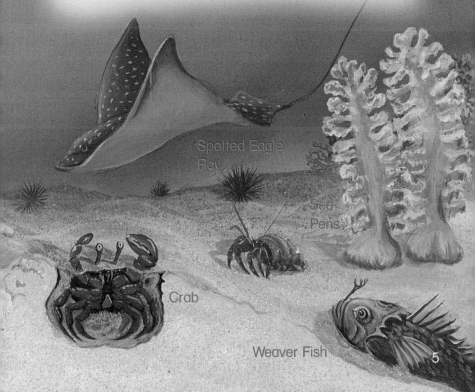

Spotted Eagle Ray

Sea Pens

Crab

Weaver Fish

Now let's go to a deeper area. Just below the ocean's surface is the sunlit zone. Divers can still see sunlight in this zone. Turtles, sharks, eels, salmon, and many other fish live in this zone. The water temperature here changes with the air temperature, since it is so close to the surface.

There isn't much mystery about this zone, but you should be wary of some of its inhabitants. You probably don't want to meet up with a shark or a man-of-war. Sharks bite, and a man-of-war can give you a nasty sting.

Strong currents help animals move around in the sunlit zone.

In the sunlit zone of tropical areas, you may also find magnificent corals and huge coral reefs. Most of a coral reef is made up of nonliving material. But the top parts of the reef are living coral. Coral comes in many shapes and colors, although much coral has a rosy hue.

Coral is interesting in itself. But it is also home to many sea creatures. Animals that live in coral reefs need the reefs for shelter. The reefs also provide algae—a food for many sea animals. The colorful reef creatures are often named for the land objects they look like. Do you think the lettuce slug, brain coral, sea fan, organ pipe, and sea cucumber are well named?

Man-of-War

Turtle

Salmon

Shark

Sea Fan

Organ Pipe

Brain
Coral

Lettuce Slug

7

It's now time to go deeper to the twilight zone. This is the next layer in the ocean. The water in the twilight zone is not as clear, since it does not receive much sunlight. If you see well at night, you might spot a giant squid or a hatchet fish. With luck, you might see a sperm whale. This whale visits a few ocean zones to feed.

Some fish in the twilight zone only stay there during daylight hours. They return to the sunlit zone at night, where they feed on the great many plants and animals living there.

In the twilight zone, many fish provide their own light shows. The hatchet fish has light organs that run along its underside. It is able to make its lights dimmer or brighter. This depends on how much light comes down from the surface. Changing its light patterns makes the hatchet fish almost invisible to its predators. When the hatchet fish approaches its prey, it opens its mouth to expose bright spots in its jaw. These bright spots lure its prey inside.

Hatchet
Fish

Are you ready to go even deeper? It's time to approach the layer of the ocean known as the dark zone. This zone holds many secrets, since it is difficult to observe. Still, researchers are learning a great deal about this dark, silent part of the ocean. Below 3,300 feet, all light from the surface disappears, water temperature is close to freezing, and few plants and animals can survive. Creatures here have adaptations that help them survive in their dark, cold home. Many of these creatures have large mouths, as well as stomachs that can hold tremendous amounts of food. Because food is scarce, they must be able to take in whatever comes along, and then store it—in case they don't eat again for a long time.

The fish in this zone are well-equipped for the darkness. For example, the gulper eel has a "tail light" which researchers believe attracts prey. The gulper eel has huge jaws that open wide enough to allow it to gulp very large fish.

The deep-sea angler has a "headlight," a rod on the top of its head that attracts prey. And the flashlight fish has two light-producing organs it can cover. When a predator swims nearby, the flashlight fish allows its light to glow as it swims quickly in a straight line. Then it covers the light and dashes away at an angle, leaving the confused predator behind.

Deep-Sea
Angler

Gulper Eel

Tripod Fish

Sea Spider

At last we've reached the very bottom of the ocean. There are no waves on the ocean floor. The temperature never warms to much above freezing. Most creatures at this depth grow very slowly, due to the scarcity of food and the cold temperature.

Since SCUBA divers can't descend to the ocean floor, how do scientists know about it? Navy researchers have gathered information about these depths through voyages in vehicles that can go down to about 13,000 feet. These vehicles are equipped with bright lights and a variety of research tools. To explore even deeper, researchers launch robot-like vehicles, since it is too dangerous for human beings at those depths.

At great depths, you might discover the tripod fish and the so-called sea spider. The tripod fish can detect the scent of prey above it. Its stilt-like fins raise it high above the floor.

The sea spider is not a true spider even though its four pairs of tall legs make it look like one. Long legs allow the sea spider to move along the ocean floor, without stirring up much soft clay and mud that might warn its prey.

In 1977, biologists in the Pacific Ocean were surprised to find giant clams, large worms, and crabs in and around deep cracks on the ocean floor. From the cracks rose black, smokey gases. These cracks are too deep for sunlight to reach. Also, there is little oxygen at this depth, and it should have been too cold for these creatures to live there. When they looked closer, the scientists found that hot-water vents warm these areas. The warm water comes from hot lava in volcanoes under the ocean floor.

What was still a question was how these creatures could survive without oxygen or any plants to eat. Scientists were surprised to learn that gases coming up from the cracks change into oxygen. The creatures can breathe this gas and it helps grow nourishment to feed them.

15

You've now explored all the layers of the ocean. And you've learned about a few of the many animals who live there. Perhaps the next time you walk along the seashore collecting shells or driftwood, you will think about the mysterious and fascinating creatures that live in oceans around the world.